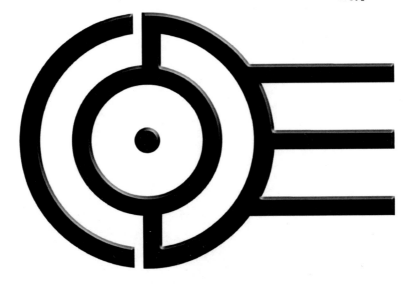

CREATIONS OF
a DIVINE ENTITY

Poetry by Taylor Code with Art by Plek One

Copyright © 2018 by Taylor Code
TX000U2096183
April 25th, 2018

Graphic layout by CalmPlex Art & Design
Illustrations by Plek One

Published by Creations of a Divine Entity

creationsofadivineentity@gmail.com

Printed in the United States of America

ISBN 978-0-692-08503-5

Foreword

For over 20 years, I've had the great privilege of witnessing Taylor Code walk the road to redemption that the poems contained in this book so brilliantly illuminate. From childhood victim to gang member to juvenile offender to prison inmate to student to teaching artist and restorative justice advocate, Taylor has taken what he jokingly refers to as "the scenic route to enlightenment." Jokes aside, it is a great blessing for us all that he brought a pencil and notebook along to document his epic journey home.

Taylor is a gifted wordsmith in service to soul, a wounded healer packing poetic medicine for our nation's next generation of youth. His poems open doors to depths that few can fathom, and windows to visions that promise to feed our dreams. They reflect the reality of an old soul's young life lived hard and fast, marked by dramatic initiatory thresholds and sometimes surprising humor and beauty. Taylor's poems dig deep through concrete streets and cell blocks to the ancestral roots that ultimately connect us to the earth and to each other. As someone who has witnessed the impact of his poetry on thousands of at-risk youth and adults over the years, I can say with confidence that these poems are literally life-saving works of art, with the power to reach and move those buried behind even the hardest protective shells.

Taylor Code's Creations of a Divine Entity should be entered into with caution and respect for the transformational force of what lies inside. If you're stuck in life and determined to stay that way, this book is probably not for you. If, on the other hand, you're looking for inspiration for your own healing journey, or if you're interested in an antidote to the cycles of violence and addiction that continue to plague our schools, prisons and communities, open wide! You're about to embark on one hell of a ride.

Christopher Henrikson
Founder, Street Poets Inc.

"IN A DARK TIME, THE EYE BEGINS TO SEE"

— Theodore Roethke

Pops

Taylor Code lives on

Poppa was a rollin stone
Wherever you laid your hat
That was your home

You had to be the inspiration
For that song
'Cuz rarely did I see you without
Some type of crown on your dome
When you were finally called home
I'm sure you strutted through the gates
Like a king to his throne
With that mischievous grin across your face
You loved simple things in life
Like black walnut ice cream
When you watched the horse races at night
On that zenith black and white

"Your eyes may shine
Your teeth may grit
But none of this
Will you get"
Your teasing bit

Diddy was your moniker
Your homies called you Hammer
Tactics slick enough
To con a gentleman out of his manners
A sharp method to your madness
But Moms wasn't having it
She'd kick down the door
Wielding a skillet from the cabinet
A match made in heaven
Trapped in the belly of the beast
Gave birth to a seed
Who's unapologetically a G

Never knew the ghosts from your past
Would haunt you to the bone
I was too traumatized by the pain
Of facing the world alone
But from this moment on
I shall weep no more
You and Mama can rest easy
Your son's back from the war

Poppa was a rollin stone
Wherever you laid your hat
That was your home

You had to be the inspiration
For that song
'Cuz I ain't stopped hearing it
Since I got word you was gone

My sister Janet was a straight up G

She once beat the brakes off a girl
The girl's mother
And her big brother
One by one
Like Louis Gossett Jr.
In the movie *Diggstown*
Just lined 'em all up
And dug deep in that ass
When her boyfriend made the mistake
Of giving her some cheap earrings for her birthday
Concealed between five one dollar bills
She nearly severed a significant
Portion of flesh
From the left side of his chest with her teeth
And I can still hear him screaming
As she pinned him on the couch
Cussed him the hell out
Rage barely escaping
The blood stained teeth in her mouth
But it wasn't the earrings
That drove her over the edge
It was the way that Mr. Lackadaisical
Said he'd forgotten to get her a card
As if his gift
Was more than enough to compensate
For why he deserved her love
In the first place
My sister wasn't a maniac
Violence was just her response to heartache
So after she busted him in his kneecaps
With my silver aluminum baseball bat
And told me to get the butcher knife
From the dishwater in the kitchen sink
I retrieved it before she could blink
I didn't wanna be the next dude responsible for breaking her heart
Plus I was a lot smaller than I am now
And though I'm about two feet taller
180 pounds heavier
Than the nine year old boy
Those big girls
Jacked for his trick or treat candy
I still remember how she
Cut 'em off at the alley
Stretched my dad's 12-gauge across the roof of the car
To save her teary eyed little brother's Halloween
My sister was all heart

My muscle
My queen

I am He

GIVEN LIFE
I AM HE
I AM HE WHO
GIVEN LIFE BY
THE MOMENT THE
OVER BLOOD WARM
INTO A

I am he who has been given life
By way of death
The moment the Middle Passage opened
Over blood warm water
Into a hurricane of pain
I set sail
Stripped of my name and African tongue
Through the battle of Gettysburg
Beyond the infamous boycotts of the South

My soul shipwrecked on the shores of Los Angeles
When people stopped fighting with fists
But started shooting to kill
The most undesirable parts of themselves
And since I resembled so many
Seven bullets have found their home
In my plantation branded flesh

I am he who has been given life
By way of death
Through the stress of a broken nest
Dad a slave to opium dreams
Mom arguing with people she can't see
Sisters birthing children of their own
Death and me have been tight
Since I was three

I am he who has been given life
By way of death
Fear buried in my tear-stained pillow
Peers ostracized me
For not having cool shoes
I stopped going to class
So the streets became school

I've been the fool who trades gold
For that which depreciates with time
The hustler who hustles himself
Slangin' quarters for a dime

I am he who has been given life
By way of death
So I humbly manifest
Appreciation for the gift
Of each and every breath

Face Off

I knew I wouldn't be
A *Toys R Us* kid forever
But how the hell did I go
From *Hulkamania* to *Thug Life*
BMX freestyles to berettas?

Whatever got me buzzed
When those riots broke out
Sparked a fire in my lungs
That hasn't allowed me to breathe
Since '91

Dead man walking

A phrase tailor-made
To fit my existence
Like the shoes that I wear
When I just wanna mob around this prison

All this reminiscin bout the good 'ol days
Got me laughin at the way
I once wooed a girl
By singing her the theme song to
Growing Pains

Yeah
That was me
Flying up the street
In a milk crate nailed to my skateboard
In pursuit of imaginary crooks
For robbing that make believe liquor store

One-Adam-12
I have a visual on the suspect
He's hiding in my mirror
And it ain't like we just met

The sparkle in his eyes
Is familiar yet distant
"They'll never take me alive"
He pledges without blinking

Smoke Screen

I've walked through fire
With no fire proof suit
And returned unburned
Now what yall wanna do
Poised to shock the world
As if my name was Cassius
Beating ya brakes off
With poetic like lashes
Blasphemous bastards
Ain't ready for the pain
So step your game down
And hop back in your lane
The epiphany to your blindness
In exchange for your soul
The rawness of the rhyme
Holds value like gold
The world is a hustle
Rules all rearranged
Culture vultures strip you of everything
From your God to your name
They got the nerve to tell lies
Though we televise the ugly truth
I only got one question
What's left for us to do
Jewels buried in my bones
Like a long lost treasure
Exploding on the mic
Like a pipe under pressure
With pleasure I give you
The most uncut version
'Cuz it's heavy on my heart
And I need to lift the burden
There's a demon in my essence
And you all know who
Be sure that you read
All the signs in the zoo
Karma is the fate
That only pays what you earn
If you play with the fire
Don't hate it when you burn

But the hard way is the only way
Most of us learn
Lost in the madness
While the world still turns
Third eye closed
Like the banks on Sunday
Driving the wrong way
Down a one lane runway
It's hard to be my brother's keeper
When he keeps heat for me
To blast me out my boots
And leave me sleep eternally
Fear not though I walk
In the shadow of death
Crows will carry my soul to the throne
To get rest
Prophecies undoubtedly
Reveal what is coming
Brush that dirt off your heart
Ain't you tired of running
A picture of the future
Your lifestyle beholds
Now break out your tickets
Welcome to the show
It's murder and mayhem
Dishonesty involved
We the have-nots
Are just pawns in it all
Did it dawn on you at all
That it's all just a fraud
A straight smokescreen
To keep us blind to the cause
Rape and deceit
Greed in it all
We the have-nots
Mislead in it all
Did it dawn on you at all
That it's all just a fraud
A straight smokescreen
To keep us blind to the cause

Bottom Line

Eternal struggles trying to bubble up
And hustle for my dreams
Off crack sacks
Car jacks
And criminalistic schemes
Razor blade sharades
Baggies and triple beam scales
Ready to set up shop
Hit the block and clock sales

Grew up seeing Pops
Shoot smack and stack bread
Passing out in dirty clothes
Like he was half past dead
Born addicted to psych meds
Cause Moms had mental issues
Sisters with kids of their own
I couldn't help but feel alone

Started to roam these cold streets
Amongst lost souls and thugs
Only twelve years old
When I started to smoke bud
So heart broke from the hardships
I was driven to start shit
Wasn't blessed with skillful hands
So at first I got my ass kicked

Mad 'cuz Dad wouldn't
Teach me the dope game
And I know he's at least
Touched a few keys of cocaine
The trials and tribulations
Manifesting in this song
Is not meant to glorify
The shit I did wrong

How could any man breathing
Let his son stand on his own
From the time he was born
Til he got to prison
I don't know
Where the fuck were you
When I was young
Wild and restless
Flipped the script with the homies
Now I'm thugged out with a death wish

I love you to death
But I will never understand
How you left me and Mama
For that glass dick so quick and fast
All the teachers at my school
Think I'm fifty-one fifty
I'm really a fuckin genius
It's just without you I feel empty

Gave me your first and last name
And it was a wrap after that
I had to hunt you down in traffic
Like you ran off with my sack
Moms tried to compensate
For the flaws in your position
But the pain was too much
I said fuck it
And got with the business
Robbed innocent people
Of rent money and foodstamps
With my goons from the turf
And got shipped me off to boot camp

Now my only hope for the future
Is to boss up with this rap shit
So I ain't gotta sing
Some sad ass I ain't have a dad shit

Twenty-six years old
On the third year of my bid
Walking the main line
Thinking about life as a kid
Only seven years old
When my sister took me to county jail
To see you behind the glass
Trapped in a man's living hell
Too young to understand
That would soon be my future
Cause I ain't got a jumpshot
Nor knowledge of computers

Schooled to be a loser
But refused the facts of life
Robbed banks in broad daylight
Sold blow sacks at night
Too deep in the streets now
To let go of all the greed
But all my daughter wanted
Was to be kissed
Held and squeezed

Damn - I'm so much like you
I never realized myself
So I'm crying through this pen
Hoping I still have a soul
Despite all my sins

Your friend's son
Cocked a burner in my face
And squeezed the trigger
But it didn't seem to matter
'Cuz you was still cool with the nigga
So long I had to carry
The burden of all that rage
That I fucked around and caught a murder case
On the front page

Was my birth a tragic accident
That ruined all your plans
Is that the damn reason you couldn't
Teach me to be a man
No matter how much this song cries
I just can't deny
I'll always be your son
And that's the bottom line

Like You

How can the son of a lost tribe
Ever find his way home
When the world sells him lies
And he fears the unknown
Righteous down to the bone
But condemned a bad seed
The pain of a broken soul
Broadcast in 3D
They wanna exile and execute us all
Like Troy Davis
Pray to the spirits
For the miracles that can save us
Haters hate
That I spit it so raw
'Cuz their character is stepped on
Like crystal meth cut with salt
Saw demons in my dreams
So I slept with the burner
Woke up in county jail
Conspiracy to a murder
Daughter crying on the sheets
Asking where is her dad
While the DA screams
"I want the chair for his ass!"
Your Honor buried me alive
Inside a concrete tomb
But I chose life over death
My spirit came anew
Stanzas took flight
Through the US Postal Service
And helped me reach beyond the walls
To reconnect with my purpose
If I was accused of crimes against humanity
Like Arabs and Israelites
Would you persecute me as the villain
'Cuz I ain't perfect like Christ
Break the ice and sacrifice
The reservations you may hold
And postpone the verdict
'Til the story's been told
Some of us walk a dark path
Before we're touched by the light
Nearly every saint you can name
Has a past as the bad guy
So who are you to pass judgement
And outcast me from society
When I'm just sticking to the script
That the universe provided me

I was blided by the shine
Of a princess cut diamond
Forgive me if I didn't show any
Remorse for being grimy
But the cloth from which I'm cut
Doesn't come from exotic places
I was just a renegade
In pursuit of big faces
Mesmerized by a dream
Surrounded by pickett fences
'Til the windows all exploded
And shattered that shallow vision
When I perish
Cherish these words like a eulogy
It is what it is
There's nothing more the world can do to me
Lock my demons in a casket
With two pounds of sage
And send them up the river
To the Lady of the lake
So she can wash the dirt away
From the portal of my wounds
And I see past the pain enough
For the gift to come through
Fact that I'm eligible for forgiveness
Is a miracle
I gave guns to boys
To drive my enemies hysterical
Unbearable as it is
My reflection in the mirror
With a face full of tears
Makes the picture seem clearer
Beneath the surface of the scars
Is the me I yearn to be
That nigga thuggin hard
Was the me I learned to be
Sent a man in the bank
With a plot to get the dough
But it turned out to be
The dude's suicide note
When my baby mama left me
Kickin rocks on the yard
Spirit still blessed me
With the breath to go hard
To sum it up with one line
One time for the youth
Lil homie slow it down
'Cuz this me could be you

I'm the product of psych meds
Smack and cocaine
In the land of the scandalous
Where even smokers got game
Hope you got a brain
'Cuz it's ill in the field
Some kill for the fame
And pop pills for the thrill
Let's keep it real for a minute
And recognize the facts
Bills have been implemented
To crucify us Blacks
So many Native tribes died
At the hands of politicians
It's damn near impossible
To find and rebuild 'em
They even wanna keep Latinos
South of the border
Just ask the homie Jorge
Who was snatched and deported

A quarter of a key
Is your lane to street fame
But its sharks in the water
That'll murk you for that thang
Freedom comes with a price
That too few can pay
'Cuz we're all brainwashed
To some degree of a slave
The greatest lie ever told
Was that the devil don't exist
So look in the mirror
If you ain't feelin this
They ain't never walked a mile
Wearing my kinda shoes
They grew up with silver spoons
While I played with the goons
And just as soon as they
See my dark face on the news
They call me a monster
But deep down I got issues like you

78054

NEVADA DEPARTMENT OF CORRECTIONS

Life is an ocean of emotion
With waves that never end
Beauty can be found in everything
Especially within
The only standards there are to live by
Are those you set for yourself
Be responsible for your own happiness
Don't stress trying to impress

Invest your energy into the endeavors
You love, breathe and dream
Make friends with people who are smarter than you
There's no limit what y'all will do
Keep your eyes on the prize
No matter how hard the times get
The pictures we paint ourselves
Determine the lives we're left with

Be humble when you win
Have grace in the face of defeat
Both ups and downs are included with the package
That's just how it's meant to be
Everything that glitters ain't gold
Don't be star struck by the shine
The real jewels are beneath the surface
Blind to many eyes

Honor your higher power
By living in your truth
Don't be afraid to stand alone
Even when the masses think less of you
And last but not least
Make use of the pen and pad
Always and forever
Your dear old dad

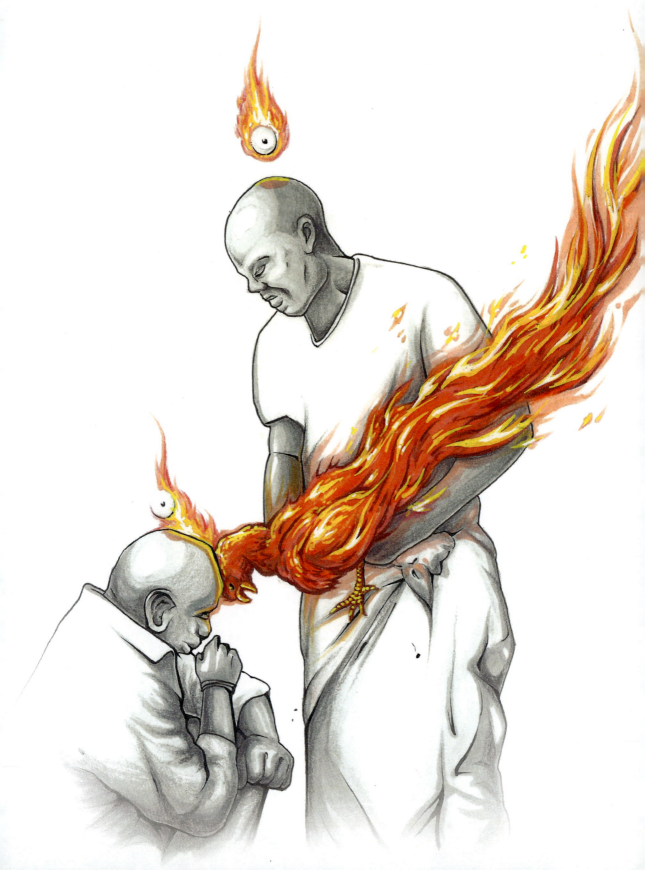

I found the key to free my soul
From the prison of history's lies
A shaman sprinkled me with dust
And opened my other eye

Everything I thought I knew
Barely scratched the surface of the truth
So I popped the red pill
And asked Orisa to see me through

The *Matrix* was a metaphor
For indigenous magic
Software the oppressor
Purposely kept us from having

Didn't realize my wings worked
'Til I fell from grace
And rose like a phoenix
In spite of all the shame and heartache

Cast a stone into the river
Let the ripples carry your intention
Out to the universe
Oh- and did I mention

An act of sacrifice
When the storm comes ashore
Can alleviate worries
And bless you to the core

Magic that won't be denied
Just read between the lines
Recipes for healing
Don't get lost in the rhyme

Medicinals and rituals
Created in sacred space
Prescribed by my doctor
Absolutely not the FDA

Political refugees
And gang affiliates of America
Have-nots and run aways
All products of the area
Capitalism
Sexism
Racism
Hate
Manufactured schemes
To keep sheep in their place
Caught a beef in the State
'Cuz I was fast and too furious
Drifting in Tokyo
'Cuz the po-po was curious
The purest of the truth
Just waiting to exhale
Like a fiend who took a blast
Of that Peruvian fish scale
Intel so elevated
It got me living with the stars
But not in Hollywood
I'm talking Venus, Pluto, Mars
Bars like Hershey's chocolate
Stop it
I'm the greatest
Perished in the matrix
But I reincarnated
Came to grips with the past
And a closet full of demons
Now the future's looking bright
And smells a lot like freedom
That's sixteen down
Thirty-two more to go
Brace yourselves folks
This is uncut dope
I give hope to lost souls
But keep none for myself
'Cuz I'm here on borrowed time
Like life after death
Can you calculate your steps
And walk your path simultaneously
If you ever learn to do it
You can claim to be the same as me
Wait a minute
Scratch
Retract that last statement
I'm the last of a dying breed
History in the making

A mid-life crisis
Twenty years before its time
Is the caption that they use
About the casualties of my rhymes
When they ask you who sent me
You all simply just reply
"That's not a torpedo
It's Taylor Code the Don"
If it ain't raw don't buy it
Let it rot on the shelf
Time to take the game back
To its purest form of wealth
Another bankable production
That's been stewing in the fire
Now all that's left to do
Is get it cosigned by Tyra
I disappeared seven years
Like I faked my own death
Now I'm back amongst my peers
With gold in my flesh
Left those glory days behind
To spread truth to my peeps
'Cuz social transformation
Will help set the world free
Nowadays it pays to be
All watered down and fake
But I keep it so gutter with these bars
That they leave permanent scars
Got a fetish for fast cars
I'm the black Ricky Bobby
Doing a hundred in the gutter lane
Bout to smash something Mami
They try to link me to conspiracies
'Cuz they clearly can't fade me
I can do it all solo
Thanks to the tribulations that made me
An overdose of truth
Mr. President regroup the troops
And compensate 'em all
To do nothing but build schools
Prison ain't designed to save lives
Nor rehabilitate the criminal
It's all about the dollar signs
And creating sicker individuals
I ain't one to gossip
So you ain't heard this from me
They say it costs to be the boss
But that's just the price of being free

I've had my eye in your direction
The very second I felt your vibe
Which happened to be so pleasant
It made me feel alive
On my side of the tracks
It ain't too many like you
Who embody the grace of a Goddess
In the style that you do
Ms. Crazy
Sexy
Cool
Don't be alarmed by my approach
I've fallen deep under your spell
So I'm here to let you know
It's salvation for my soul
To serenade you with this poem
Heaven lives in you
Paradise is in your bones
Can't believe you're all alone
Without a man to call your own
Dudes busy chasing fool's gold
When you're supposed to have the throne
I know I'm a little younger
But I've lived at least twice
So I recognize the blessing
When she arrives in my life
Nights I spend without you close enough
To hear my heart speak in tongue
Got me all discombobulated
Damn - what have you done
I know one thing for certain
Two things fa sho
You're the pot of gold
At the end of the rainbow
And although I'm still rough around
My edges and my core
My capacity to shine
Is a thousand times more
I wanna put hickies inside your thighs
A night full of ecstasy
The nectar of forbidden fruit
Just brings out the best in me

It's like you climbed off the pages
Of an exotic fairy tale
To mix fantasy and reality
In a smooth cocktail
So call me an alcoholic
'Cuz I ain't left the bar yet
Still drinking in your beauty
To the rhythm of how you step
Everybody slept on you girl
And left you all alone
'Cuz I got the key to the treasure
You've been waiting to bring home
I walk the beach all alone
Hoping to find you under the moon
The misery of being without you
Is like living in a tomb
Used to assume you wouldn't have me
Cuz of all the dirt on my hands
But you saw past all that
To see me for who I really am
Baby take my hand
As we walk across the threshold
The world is ours
As long as we don't fold
Let's live it up and lay low
Manifest an abundance of pesos
And keep it on the up
Without violating the trust
I ain't rushin you to crush
Love ain't all about lust
You can tell I know that
Just by the passion in my touch
Been up for two days
Formulating the words to this flow
'Cuz my heart speaks a code
That the mind doesn't know
But you broke it down the best
With a quick and simple quote

"The best soundtrack to love
Is a beating heart, yo"

Not too Many

I got so much rage in the bank
I'm living large off the interest
An investment trust account
Reaping the perks of big business
But before I self destruct
And let the wealth tear me apart
Let me splurge for a minute
And get this burden off my heart

I don't know how to start
'Cuz it's dark and runs deep
Back to that demon I first saw
When my parents were both sleep
I swear it only seems
Like it was just yesterday
When Pops threw Mama in the tub
With blood gushing from her face

That was a quarter century ago
But I'm still hearing screams
In my cell yelling "NO"
'Cuz they echo in my dreams
Mama took me off to Texas
When the dope took you under
And it was there I got molested
And my sunshine turned to thunder

Reflecting on these troubles
Sometimes my tears become laughs
'Cuz you had the nerve to wonder why
I chose to walk a dark path
My last hope was the streets
So I banged the local gang
But that even took something
I can never again claim

Can the Lord blame me
For all the sins I've committed
Or close the pearly gates
'Cuz I lacked the wisdom to do different
I wanted the world to feel
The kinda pain I was feeling
So I robbed and pistol whipped a man
In front of his own children

And to make matters worse
Homies showed me love for that
Celebrating all the hate
That I now wish I could take back
Was it the Haldol and Cogentin
That ran through Mama's veins
Mixed with the dope in Daddy's seed
That made me grow to be insane?

When I felt the urge to change
My enemies cashed me out with slugs
And left me leaking in the street
Talking to God about peace
My scars tell a story
That only pauses for effect
As I choke off the gun smoke
Praying to take another breath

I'd be lying if I said
I never cried in my cell
'Cuz I'm forced to face the truth
Walking the main line in jail
It's hell to be alone
And prevail against these thoughts
But I'm thankful for the chance
'Cuz I was way too lost

If I had to formulate the words
To explain the world to my daughters
It'd probably take some Hail Marys
And a fifth of Holy Water
Am I wrong for dying to tell 'em
The ugly truth we all hide
Or should I keep my mouth shut
And hope they find a way to rise

I treasure times like this
When the truth invades my spirit
But the sad thing is...

Not too many wanna hear it

From the unforgiving streets
To the land of pipe dreams
The City of Angels
Is much more than a night scene

Might seem a little biased
'Cuz I'm loyal to the soil
If you score big in L.A.
You go from common to royal

Blood used to boil
Anticipating to get the rock
So I could be like Mike
Instead of a victim to the block

Been hitting gates since elementary
To run games on the weekend
Staying out of the penitentiary
Meant having the right place to be in

Venice Beach be the spot
To showcase heart stopping moves
Hip-Hop be the platform
To drop body rockin tunes

So if you're ever in the hood
When it's a little past dark
You can still catch the up and coming ballers
at the neighborhood park

Sparks fly from the kicks
When dude cross like A.I.
And back pedal down the court
Blowing a kiss like "Hey Ma!"

Don't judge this book by its cover
Nothing is ever what it seems
Ain't a defense alive
That can lock down my dreams

Author's Note

Poetry has liberated my soul from the forces of darkness that landed me in prison for close to seven years. I didn't truly experience the power of truth and vulnerability until I was behind bars. Not knowing exactly where to start to heal, let alone the method I'd use to 'fix' myself, I simply began writing poems about the chain of events that sent me on a collision course with the big house. This process of unpacking all the trauma, shame, rage and guilt I was carrying gave me the capacity to forgive myself for my misdeeds. I was also able to access lots of good memories buried in my life, which helped to humanize me again.

Once those huge burdens were lifted from my shoulders, I realized prison existed inside me long before I was ever physically held in one. Going forward, my work would be about allowing myself to dream a lifestyle totally different from the nightmare I had lived up until that point. I owe this project to the Universe for blessing me to make it to the light at the other end of the tunnel.

My friend and graffiti artist/graphic designer, Plek One, created the illustrations in this book. He and I are two of the original six members of the Street Poets performance group of the late 90's. The art is based on real pictures taken from different periods in my life. The vision was to infuse some very personal mementos with the essence of the culture of the aforementioned journey in order to create a well-rounded experience for the reader. That being said, I hope every reader is inspired to proceed and dream the life they really want to have.

Truly,
Taylor Code

IAMTAYLORCODE.COM

For my mother, Ethel Mae.
October 21st, 1943 - June 22nd, 2000

Acknowledgements

ALL Praise to the CREATOR! Any light that emanates from me is a reflection of you.

THANK YOU to my ancestors, and all those who came before me. You walked the line and stood up under extreme atrocities, making it possible for us to have the kind of lives we have today. When I leave this realm, I hope I am worthy enough to have my name mentioned with yours.

LOVE to my parents, Ethel Mae Maxie and Taylor Code Maxie, Sr., I know you are with me even as you are resting.

Destiney, Taylor III, Tylor and Bailey - you are my EVERYTHING.

Marjorie, I love you with all my being. Thank you for your patience, for inspiring and consistently challenging me to be a better man.

I can't emphasize enough how blessed I've been on this journey. I am tremendously grateful and honored to have people in my life who can see past my mistakes, and still remain supportive and encouraging. Your kind, forgiving spirits have definitely fueled my inspiration for this project, as well as future ones.

THANK YOU: Chris Henrikson & Susannah Grant, Raven & Dexter Auston, Janet Maxie & JT Thomas, Dr. Carole Berotte Joseph, Claudine Joseph, Awo Fasegun, Leanne Whitney, Kaile Schilling, Kenneth O. Maxie Sr., Chris Abani, and BaBa Oshitola

LOVE to my Cali fam: Stephanie Maxie & Gregory Alexander Sr., Stephen Clark, Joffrey Alexander, Gregory Alexander, Jr., Sommer Maxie, Jammare Columbus, Currancie, Asante, Elijah, Quincy, Monique, Christine and Lady Bug.

LOVE to my Texas fam: Ben & Marie Montanez, Victoria & Lucille Roberts, Jason & Aisha Montanez, Jahsh, Jordan, Nia, Jon Jon, Adonis and Yasira Sonnier, Howard Prince II, Al White, Maxine Lemon, Carolyn Kelley Johnson and all the Maxie's, where ever they may be.

PEACE to all the homeboys and homegirls from the turf . One Luv fo tha EL DUB.

MUCH LOVE to my bro Anthony Rivera. Always there at the drop of a hat.

MAJOR SALUTE to Keasu`c Hill for lighting the fire I needed to make this project happen.

BIG RESPECT to: 2PAC, NAS, ICE CUBE, LL COOL J, SNOOP DOGG, SCARFACE and the many other Hip-Hop legends that inspired me to express my truth, anger, joy, pain and love.

BIG UPS to **PLEK ONE**! You're **EXTRA NICE** at what you do. It has been an absolute pleasure creating this project with you.

ENDLESS LOVE to the STREET POETS Community! Immediate and extended.

MAD PROPS to A.R.C.!

IAMTAYLORCODE.COM

Made in the USA
Lexington, KY
15 October 2018